PTUI!

HERE COMES

SNOOPY

Selected Cartoons From

SNOOPY Vol. I

by Charles M. Schulz

CORONET BOOKS
HODDER FAWCETT LTD

Copyright 1955, 1956, by United Feature Syndicate, Inc.
Copyright © 1957, 1958, by United Feature Syndicate, Inc.
First published by Fawcett Publications Inc., New York.
CORONET BOOKS EDITION 1968
Second impression 1968
Third impression 1969

SBN 340 04295 8

Printed in Great Britain for Hodder Fawcett Ltd., St. Paul's House,
Warwick Lane, London, E.C.4 by Hazell Watson & Viney Ltd.,
Aylesbury, Bucks

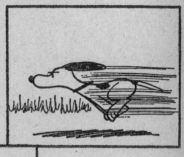

SCHULZ

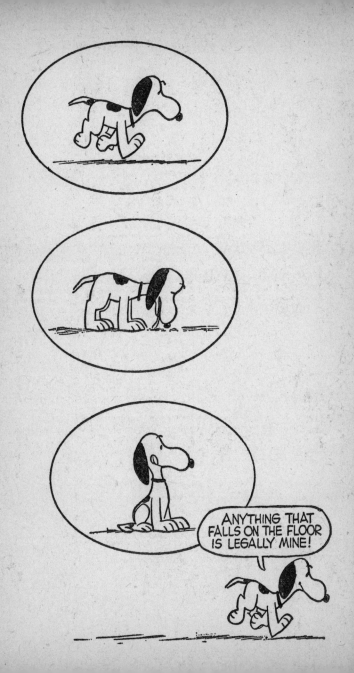

SHUDDER!

HE WAS EATING ANIMAL CRACKERS AND.. AND...AND.. **SMILING**!!

PTUI!

SCHULZ

INDECISION IS AN AWFUL THING..

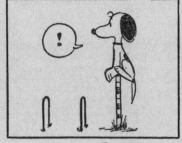

BONK

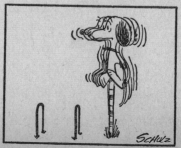

ZOOM!

NOW, YOU CUT THAT OUT!

SCHULZ

KLUNK! BUMP! BUMP! bumpety-bump CRASH!!

WHAT IN THE WORLD WAS **THAT**?!

I GUESS IT WAS SNOOPY...IF HE DOESN'T LIKE HIS SUPPER, HE JUST PUSHES IT DOWNSTAIRS!

SCHULZ

ZIP!

PHOOEY! I DIDN'T MIND NOT GETTING ANY CANDY, BUT I DIDN'T LIKE THAT REMARK, 'KINDLY REMOVE YOUR HAIRY FACE!'

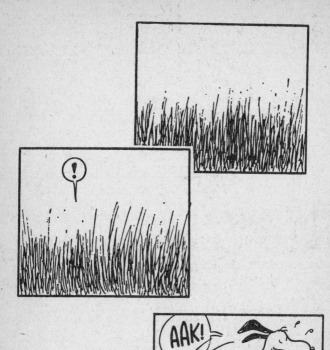

I THOUGHT I TOLD YOU TO STOP THAT DANCING?! YOU HAVE NO RIGHT TO BE SO HAPPY!!! NOW, STOP IT! DO YOU HEAR ME?!

SCHULZ

THERE SURE ARE A LOT OF WORMS ON THE SIDEWALK AFTER IT RAINS..

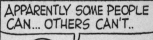